Killer Copywriting, How to Write Copy That Sells

William Swain

Can I Ask You a Quick Favor?

If you like this book, I would greatly appreciate if you could leave an honest review

Reviews are very important to us authors, and it only takes a minute to post.

Download Audio

This book is also available now as an audiobook.
Head over to www.audible.com or
Download on the Audible application

The Free Offer

Do you want to boost your sales, save time and grow your business at a lightning speed?

Start Now, and Take Your Copywriting to The Next Level

http://killercopy.ontrapages.com/

Contents

INTRODUCTION

Welcome to Operation: Killer Copywriting.

Your mission, should you choose to accept it, is to create compelling content, and learn how to sell any product or service thrown your way through the power of words.

Consider this your secret weapon.

Armed with this e-book, you have three targets to command and conquer:
- Target 01: Discover the key elements of good copy.
- Target 02: Master the secrets of conversion-driven writing.
- Target 03: Apply best practices in real business scenarios and accomplish all the free drills and exercises.

Should you be caught producing boring, irrelevant, or worse – plagiarized content – we will disavow any knowledge of your actions or purchase of this e-book.

This copy will never self-destruct and will be embedded in your brain as the most awesome introduction you've ever read.

Good luck!

CHAPTER 1: THE BASICS

Before you jump in to slaying your first winning headline or ad copy, let's cover a few basics first. In this chapter, you'll understand the importance of developing effective copywriting skills, the goal of a good copy, and the mind-blowing role of a great copywriter.

In the next chapters, you'll discover the proven strategies and tactics of copywriting, and learn how to apply best practices to real business scenarios. Just trust the process, have fun along the way, and we'll have you killing it in no time!

But first...

What is Copywriting?

Simply put, copywriting is the process of using words to make things sell better. What does this mean exactly? Let's break it down, shall we?

- **The process** – Yes, first and foremost, copywriting is a process. Unfortunately, it isn't about jumping straight to the writing part and simply putting a few words together. You first need to understand the channel or medium you're writing for, identify your goal, and study your target audience. How you write and what you write will heavily depend on these three factors – Don't worry, we'll guide you through every step of the way.

- **Using words** – Carefully chosen words can trigger an emotional response and spark your desired reaction from your target audience. Your copy needs to move them – excite them, scare them, touch them, shock them, inspire them. It's about knowing the power of using the right words to convince people to take a specific action, which brings us to the next phrase...

- **To sell better** – The goal of your copy, as part of any marketing strategy, is to convert. How you structure your copy can greatly influence how your audience behaves, and your simple choice of words may instantly spell the difference between a loss and a sale. You'll learn more about the power of words in the coming chapter.

That said, copywriting, by nature, is the most profitable skill to learn. So, congratulations on this investment into your current and future endeavors – wise choice, indeed!

With conversion as your goal, does this mean that copywriting is limited to ads then? Absolutely not.

Copywriting Then and Now

Before the wonderful world of the web existed, businesses would simply put up shop, possibly put out an advertisement on TV, radio, print, or OOH, explore telemarketing if needed, and maybe even direct mail. All those collaterals required copywriting.

These days, if your business isn't searchable online, you practically don't exist. And with search engines and social media networks running the show, quality content remains to be king. If you have or are thinking of putting up a business today, these are some of the things you'd probably have to consider writing copy for:

- Your branding / tagline
- Website
- Social media profiles
- Social media updates
- Social media ads
- Google ads
- Banner ads
- Video scripts
- Email marketing or newsletter
- Splash pages or sales pages
- Blog posts
- Articles for content marketing
- Infographics
- Presentations
- Industry reports
- Posters
- Flyers
- Brochures
- Proposals
- Sales letters
- Press releases
- E-books (yes, that's why we're doing this)

And the list goes on...

The more content you produce, the more chances for conversion. Great news is, this provides many work opportunities for copywriters! There's simply great demand for content, and nearly every aspect of a business requires a copywriter. Even brand guidelines, terms and conditions, and manuals need the amazing skills of copywriters! Design may be the first thing to catch someone's attention

– but it's good copy that keeps someone hooked, and moved to click, download, sign-up, inquire, call, or buy.

Importance of Copywriting

While effective copywriting is profitable for any business, it's important to note that essentially, the *skill* involved is mastering how to use the right words to elicit a certain action. It's about effective communication and the power of persuasion. Once you learn the right words to put together, and the most effective way to frame them, the application of this skill set is endless. It won't just be about selling *a product or service* better, but even selling your ideas, opinion, and *yourself* better.

Imagine the possibilities...
- Effectively sell your products and services to your customers and exceed your sales quota.
- Competently share your thoughts with your team, and have them follow your lead.
- Confidently present your ideas to your boss, and finally get that raise or promotion you've been gunning for.
- Boldly talk about your skills with your head hunter, and grab that opportunity you've been waiting for.
- Skillfully discuss your proposal with possible investors, and finally close that business deal.
- Expertly win an argument with your partner on whose fault it really is this time – Okay... Let's not push it.

Are you ready to be a Master Manipulator?

Now that we've discussed the *what's,* head over to the next chapter and we'll walk you through the exact *how's* of killer copywriting!

CHAPTER 2: THE BOOT CAMP

In the previous chapter, you were briefly introduced to the process involved even *before* you start writing. In this boot camp, you'll learn exactly how to create your content plan to keep you on track throughout your copywriting task at hand.

Start with the end in mind.

It's important to set a crystal-clear goal for yourself to give your ideas direction and keep your writing style focused. And while you may be itching to simply jump straight to writing mode, I promise you this extra step will set you up for success.

What's your plan of attack?

It all begins by asking yourself these four questions:
- Who are you talking to?
- What do you want them to *know* about your product or service?
- What do you want them to *feel* while they're reading your copy?
- What do you want them to *do* after they read your copy?

Creating a Persona

Answering the first question is easy. Who is your copy intended for? Male and female college students who may need help with certain subjects, stay at home moms searching for a convenient fitness app, or men in their 50s who want to try a new hobby? While identifying certain demographics as your target audience is often simple, creating a persona is even better.

What is a persona?
Building a user persona means going beyond just a collective age bracket, gender, or lifestyle. It's about putting a face to your target reader, stepping into their world, determining their challenges and pain points, finding out their dreams and aspirations, and spotting the opportunity of how your product or service can be what motivates them to reach their goals.

Who's the ideal person who would want your product or service? To develop a good understanding of your target customer, a little research can go a long way. Good news is, this "research" may actually be easier than you think – people are just more than willing to voice out their concerns and opinions about anything and everything these days. Just check your Facebook feed... See what I mean?

How to Get Started
It may feel a bit stalker-y at times, so best consider yourself as an undercover spy. Here are a few methods you may want to try:
- Check out social media groups and hashtags related to your topic – Those ### are dying to be clicked on! What's the general sentiment? What are people saying? What do they like and dislike about products similar to yours?
- Check out Amazon, Yelp, and other review sites that are relevant to your business. You can also browse through comments on related blog posts and videos. That's a market insight heaven right there. What are

their common challenges? Which expectations were not met?

- Talk to people similar to your target audience (your Millennial niece maybe?), or better yet, talk directly to your customers. If you already have an existing database, try reaching out for a survey or see if there are any patterns in your customers' questions and feedback.

By doing these and immersing yourself in their world, not only will you gain valuable market insights – You'll learn to use their language, too. Instead of using technical words or business jargon, you can echo their sentiments, expressions and tone in your copy. This will also help you gain their trust and respect, as they'd appreciate being spoken to in a manner they're most familiar and comfortable with.

Drill #1

Create your own persona for a new mobile phone that your client will launch next month. Here's a table you can fill out to help you get started:

Demographics	Age, gender, education, income, status?
Career Background	Industry, job, responsibility, career path?
Career Goals	More time, more income, more awards?
Personal Interests	What are their hobbies, where do they go often?

Attitude and Values	Are they health-conscious, eco-friendly, thrifty?
Challenges	What are their main frustrations?
Potential Bottlenecks	What could be their possible objections about using your product / service?

For the purpose of this exercise and the following drills throughout this e-book, here's our sample persona:

Samantha is a young professional in her early 20s. She's an associate for an events company and works directly with various clients and suppliers. She loves her job, and though it's a fast-paced industry, she finds herself still wanting to do more outside work – She needs another outlet for her creative, adventurous spirit. She's the first to try the latest trends, and post about them on her social media. Secretly, she's dying to be an IG-influencer and luckily, being in the events industry has helped her build the right connections for it. Being offline or having her phone die on her in the middle of the day is her worst nightmare – Imagine all the possible messages, calls, or IG-worthy moments she could be missing every minute she's disconnected.

By creating a persona, you can focus your research and dig deeper into your target customer's culture. The more you know about them, the better you can tailor your copy to speak directly to them. The most important points to identify are their main challenges and potential bottlenecks. Remember – your goal is to be *the* solution they've been waiting for.

Features vs Benefits

Now that you've studied your market, let's move on to the next question: What do you want them to know about your product or service? Instinctively, you might just start listing down your product features and how it's the first, the new, the best, the one, the only...

Features tell. Benefits sell.
Product features are important, they're what *literally* sets one product apart from another – Its specs, colors, materials, and so on. But it's translating these features into relevant benefits that will give your offer a competitive edge.

Instead of just listing and telling your customers all your amazing product features, it would be wiser (and a lot less boring) to sell the *results*. How will they benefit from your product? Go back to your persona and paint a picture of how your product's features will help them address their frustrations or achieve their goals.

Here's a cool trick to help you turn basic features into key benefits – Simply ask, *so what?*

So instead of saying…

> *This awesome new phone weighs only 157g, with 6.3" Quad HD+ Super AMOLED (2960 x 1440), 521 ppi infinity display. It's available in Black Pearl, Blue Coral, Black Onyx, Gold Platinum, Silver Titanium, White Pearl, and Pink Gold. It has a 4000MAh battery capacity, and comes with 128GB internal storage and 6GB RAM. Best of all, it has a Dual Camera with dual OIS – Wide-angle camera and Telephoto camera.*

Try breaking down the important features and ask yourself – so what?

- *This awesome new phone weighs only 157g*
  So what?
  It's perfect for your versatile, on-the-go and active lifestyle!

- *6.3" Quad HD+ Super AMOLED (2960 x 1440), 521 ppi infinity display*
  So what?
  You don't miss a single detail while watching and editing your videos!

- *It's available in Black Pearl, Blue Coral, Black Onyx, Gold Platinum, Silver Titanium, White Pearl, and Pink Gold*
  So what?
  You're sure to find one that perfectly suits your style!

- *It has a 4000MAh battery capacity*
  So what?
  Your phone can finally keep up with your demanding mobile lifestyle!

- *Comes with 128GB internal storage and 6GB RAM*
  So what?
  You can build and keep more memories – not delete them!

- *Best of all, it has a Dual Camera with dual OIS – Wide-angle camera and Telephoto camera.*
  So what?
  You can capture perfect moments #forthegram all day and night!

Now you have a more interesting list of solutions to sell your persona. They can then go into the specs and further details if they're interested to know more.

The Power of Words

Words have the power to cut to the core and connect with you customers on a deep emotional level. They also hold the answer to the next question on your content plan – What do you want your customers to *feel*?
The Three Most Powerful Words
Discover.
Free.

Secret.

These are some of the most powerful words used in sales as they spark a certain emotion. They make you *feel* something – excited, intrigued, or curious at the very least.

After you identify your product benefits, keep asking *so what* until you dig into an emotional benefit. What does your customer *really* care about?

Persuasive copy harnesses the power of emotion to appeal to an inner craving. What are your persona's dreams and aspirations, what do they value most? Is it fame? Power? Prestige? Security? Health?

Once you've identified this, you can add more detail to your copy and paint a clear picture that evokes a genuine feeling.

Seven Saleable Emotions

To write an even more compelling copy, try working around the seven most effective emotions to trigger:

- *Fear* – This is definitely one of, if not, the most powerful emotion you can use to hook your reader. How many times have you agreed to do or buy something simply out of fear?

- *Encouragement* – We could always use a little encouragement, especially when we're already frustrated with whatever challenges we're facing. If a product filled with hope of solving your problem suddenly pops on your feed, wouldn't that catch your attention?

- *Anger* – While some people may appreciate encouraging copy, some may respond better to a product that echoes exactly what they're feeling. They're beyond disappointed, they're absolutely mad, and they need a solution NOW!!! (Hint: That's you.)

- *Curiosity / Secrecy* – The tease of a secret or something forbidden is just too hard to resist! Feed your customer's curiosity to get that click.

- *Safety / Security* – Selling, itself, isn't the biggest challenge – It's gaining trust. Present yourself as a trust-worthy business, and you've got one foot in the door.

- *Lust* – It's no secret, sex sells. And a good copywriter can make almost anything look and sound sexy!

- *Greed* – But wait, there's more! The promise of more money, more savings, the best, the highest, and the greatest are the most overused copy points, but simply because they're still extremely effective.

So, Master Manipulator, which of these buttons would you like to push? Here are a few power words you can use to boost your copy and achieve a compelling emotional impact!

Powerful Words that Trigger Fear

Agony	Backlash	Blood	Beware
Apocalypse	Beating	Blunder	Blinded

Armageddon	Bloodbath	Bloodcurdling	Bloody
Assault	Bomb	Buffoon	Bumbling
Cadaver	Catastrophe	Caution	Collapse
Catastrophe	Cripple	Crazy	Danger
Crisis	Deadly	Destroy	Deceiving
Death	Devastating	Disastrous	Embarrass
Dumb	Drowning	Doom	Fail
Feeble	Fired	Frantic	Fooled
Fool	Frightening	Gullible	Gambling
Hack	Hoax	Hazardous	Invasion
Holocaust	Hurricane	Insidious	Injure
Horrific	Lawsuit	Jail	Jeopardy
Lawsuit	Looming	Massacre	Lurking
Lunatic	Meltdown	Mistake	Mired
Menacing	Murder	Nightmare	Pale
Painful	Panic	Peril	Pitfall
Piranha	Plague	Plunge	Plummet
Played	Poison	Prison	Poor
Pummel	Risky	Reckoning	Revenge
Refugee	Pus	Searing	Scream
Scary	Silly	Shellacking	Slaughter
Shatter	Slave	Strangle	Stupid
Tailspin	Tank	Targeted	Teetering
Terror	Terrorist	Trap	Toxic
Tragedy	Torture	Volatile	Victim
Vaporize	Vulnerable	Wounded	Worry
Warning			

Powerful Words that Trigger Encouragement

Amazing	Ascend	Astonishing	Astounding
Audacious	Awe-inspiring	Awesome	Badass

Backbone	Blissful	Belief	Beat
Brilliant	Bravery	Breathtaking	Celebrate
Cheer	Command	Colossal	Conquer
Courage	Defiance	Defeat	Daring
Dominate	Delight	Dignity	Devoted
Effortless	Empower	Excited	Excellent
Epic	Extraordinary	Eye-opening	Fabulous
Faith	Fantastic	Fearless	Ferocious
Fierce	Force	Fulfill	Glorious
Glory	Graceful	Grateful	Grateful
Guts	Happy	Heart	Hero
Hope	Honor	Incredible	Jubilant
Jaw-dropping	Legend	Life-changing	Magic
Miraculous	Miracle	Mind-blowing	Master
Marvelous	Noble	Perfect	Persuade
Phenomenal	Pluck	Power-Up	Praise
Prevail	Remarkable	Revel	Rule
Sensational	Seize	Score	Spectacular
Splendid	Spirit	Spine	Spunk
Staggering	Strengthen	Striking	Supreme
Stunning	Stunt	Strong	Surprising
Terrific	Thrive	Thwart	Titan
Tough	Tremendous	Triumph	Unbeatable
Unbelievable	Unforgettable	Unique	Unleash
Uplifting	Valiant	Valor	Vanquish
Victory	Win	Wonderful	Wondrous

Powerful Words that Trigger Anger

Abhorrent	Arrogant	Ass-kicking	Abuse
Annoying	Bash	Barbaric	Backstabbing

Blatant	Big mouth	Beat-down	Brutal
Bullshit	Bully	Cocky	Coward
Clown	Cheat	Corrupt	Clobber
Curse	Crush	Crooked	Debase
Desecrate	Delinquent	Defile	Demolish
Disgusting	Dishonest	Disgusting	Evil
Exploit	Force-fed	Full of shit	Freaking out
Full of shit	Greedy	Gross	Harass
Horrid	High and mighty	Hate	Infuriating
Jackass	Kick	Kill	Knock Out
Knock	Know it all	Livid	Lies
Loathsome	Loser	Lying	Maul
Misleading	Money-grubbing	Nasty	No Good
Nazi	Obnoxious	Oppressive	Payback
Pain in the ass	Perverse	Pest	Pesky
Phony	Pissed off	Pompous	Pollute
Pound	Punch	Pretentious	Preposterous
Punish	Rampant	Repelling	Ravage
Revile	Repugnant	Revolting	Rude
Rotten	Ruined	Ruthless	Scam
Savage	Sick and tired	Scold	Slam
Sink	Slander	Slay	Slap
Smash	Smug	Smear	Sniveling
Snooty	Snob	Spoil	Snotty
Stuck up	Suck	Terrorize	Trounce
Trash	Up to here	Underhanded	Violate
Tyranny			

Powerful Words that Trigger Curiosity

Ancient	Backdoor	Banned	Behind the scenes
Black Market	Blacklisted	Bootleg	Censored
Classified	Cloak and dagger	Concealed	Confessions
Confidential	Controversial	Covert	Cover-up
Exotic	Forbidden	Forgotten	From the vault
Hidden	Hush-hush	Illegal	Insider
Little-known	Lost	Never seen before	Off the record
Off-limits	Outlawed	Private	Restricted
Sealed	Secret	Smuggled	Strange
Tried to hide	Unauthorized	Uncensored	Under wraps
Undercover	Underground	Under-the-table	Undisclosed
Unexpected	Unlock	Unreachable	Unspoken
Unveiled	Withheld		

Powerful Words that Trigger Safety

Above and beyond	Anonymous	Authentic	Automatic
Backed	Bankable	Best-selling	Clockwork
Certified	Cancel anytime	Endorsed	Foolproof
Ironclad	Lifetime	Guaranteed	Money-back
No-fail	No risk	No questions asked	No strings attached
No obligation	Official	Professional	Permanent
Protected	Privacy	Proven	Recession-proof

Reliable	Refund	Results	Research
Risk-free	Rock-solid	Science-backed	Survive
Secure	Sure-fire	Scientific	Tested
Trustworthy	That never fails	Thorough	Try before you buy
Unconditional	World-class	Verify	

Powerful Words that Trigger Lust

	Allure	Arouse	Bare
Begging	Beguiling	Brazen	Captivating
Charm	Cheeky	Climax	Crave
Delight	Delirious	Depraved	Desire
Dirty	Divine	Ecstasy	Embrace
Enchant	Enthralling	Entice	Entrance
Excite	Explicit	Exposed	Fascinate
Forbidden	Frisky	Goosebumps	Hanker
Heavenly	Hottest	Hypnotic	Impure
Indecent	Intense	Intoxicating	Itching
Juicy	Kinky	Kiss	Lascivious
Lewd	Lick	Lonely	Longing
Love	Lure	Luscious	Lush
Lust	Mischievous	Mouth-watering	Naked
Naughty	Nude	Obscene	Orgasmic
Passionate	Pining	Pleasure	Provocative
Racy	Raunchy	Risqué	Rowdy
Salacious	Satisfy	Saucy	Scandalous
Seduce	Seductive	Sensual	Sex
Shameless	Sinful	Sleazy	Sleeping
Spank	Spellbinding	Spicy	Steamy
Stimulating	Strip	Sweaty	Tantalizing
Taste	Tawdry	Tease	Tempting

Thrilling	Tickle	Tight	Tingle
Turn on	Unabashed	Uncensored	Untamed
Untouched	Urge	Voluptuous	Vulgar
Wet	Whip	Wild	Yummy

Powerful Words that Trigger Greed

	Bank	Bargain	Best
Billion	Bonanza	Booked solid	Cash
Cheap	Costly	Discount	Dollar
Double	Explode	Extra	Feast
Fortune	Free	Freebie	Frenzy
Frugal	Gift	Golden	Greatest
High-paying	Inexpensive	Jackpot	Lowest price
Luxurious	Marked down	Massive	Money
Money-draining	Money-saving	Nest egg	Pay zero
Prize	Profit	Quadruple	Reduced
Rich	Savings	Six-figure	Skyrocket
Soaring	Surge	Treasure	Triple
Waste	Wealth	Whopping	

Drill #3

Now that you're equipped with power words, let's go back to your persona and our sample phone product benefits. This time, ask *so what* again, choose a value you want to address, and an emotion you'd like to trigger. Finally, draft an emotional benefit and amplify them with some power words!

Here's an example of the different ways you can sell the phone's *4000MAh battery capacity*. Complete the table with four more emotional benefits.

Product Benefit	Goals / Value	Emotion	Emotional Benefit
This phone can finally keep up with your demanding mobile lifestyle!	Connections, Time, Wants to be an IG Influencer	Fear	What if your phone fails you again when you need it most?
		Greed	Don't waste a single minute to build another connection.
		Encouragement	Make every day, epic.

Making your target audience feel something is key. The more you know about them, the better you can shape your copy to spark the right emotion.

And now that they're hooked, you can finally answer the last question – What do you want them to *do*?

Compelling Calls to Action

Now this last bit is often the simplest, but most overlooked part of a content plan. Sometimes, you may assume your reader should obviously click on your copy, and that you clearly want them to buy already – but do you really want to leave that to chance?

Your readers are bombarded with creative and exciting offers every day, and they may easily just look away for a second and click on something else. Simply adding that extra word, phrase or button may be all the reminder they need to close the deal. Keep your copy foolproof, and make conversion as easy and effortless as possible with a compelling call to action.

How to Write an Effective Call to Action (CTA)

While a simple "click here" or "call now" may do the trick, here are some other surefire ways to phrase your call to action. Explore different styles and see which works best for your product, service and offer.

- **Be direct** – Keep it short and simple. This is where your *click here* and *call now* would fall under, together with the *sign-up here* and *download now*. Absolutely nothing wrong with these! Sometimes, readers just need to know where to click.

- **Make it interesting** – You could also add the emotional benefit to make your CTA more appealing. There's always room to make your copy more creative, personal and relevant to your target audience. *Click here to start making every day epic.* Or *Call now for a brighter future, today.*

- **Use power words** – As covered in The Power of Words section earlier, these are scientifically-proven words that compel customers to action. These include *new, discover, free, act now*, and the extensive list from the previous chapter. If you combine power words with your emotional benefit, you could say *Click here and discover how you can make every day epic.*

- **Sound urgent** – Aside from adding *now* or *today* in your CTAs, you could also hint at having a limited time or a limited number of items for your offer. Adding phrases like *don't miss out* or *before it's all gone* should do the trick. Again, you could also be more creative and say *Sign-up now before someone steals your spot* or *Buy now while we still have this in your size!*

- **Remove the risks** – Gaining your target audience's trust can be challenging, especially if they're just hearing about your business for the first time. They may be really interested, and just need some form of assurance to help put their hesitation at bay. To make your CTA more appealing, you can throw in a risk-free clause with your offer. *Sign-up now for your free 30-day trial. Subscribe now and cancel anytime.* Phrases like *no credit card needed* and *full money back guarantee* are also all-time favorites for a reason. They simply work!

Drill #4

Try to write at least 10 creative calls to action that relate to your samples from Drill #3. Don't forget to explore different styles and combinations of power words!

Remember, the ultimate goal of any sales copy is conversion – and a compelling call to action is the last piece of the puzzle your readers need to complete their transaction.

Now jump to the next chapter to discover the secrets of killer copywriting, before others beat you to it!

CHAPTER 3: THE BIG GUNS

You've finally mapped out your plan of action. You've gained valuable insights about your persona, you've identified their pain points and how your product benefits are the answer, you've selected an emotion you believe they'll best connect with, and you have the right power words to trigger them to follow your clear call to action.

Now it's time to put all those key elements together, and start writing!

In this chapter, you'll finally get your hands dirty and learn the
the proven formulas, strategies and tactics of effective copywriting. So, gear up and get ready to take on the big guns. It's open season!

Scientifically-Proven Copywriting Formulas

Did you ever wish there was just a formula you could simply follow to produce effective copy? There is. There are quite a few, actually, and you're about to meet the two women on top – AIDA and PAS.

AIDA
AIDA has long been known to be the princess of copywriting. She's been in the business for so long – since the 1900s – that you should just consider her to be *the queen* of copywriting. She rules when it comes to presenting product benefits, in an interesting way.

AIDA stands for Attention, Interest, Desire, and Action, and here's how you can make her the star of your copy:

- **Attention** – Start with a bold headline. As an ancient queen, AIDA lives by the old saying, go big or go home. Start with a bang to immediately get your reader's attention, then teasingly lure them in to your lair.
- **Interest** – Now that you got your target's attention, present them with your product benefits. Why do they need your product, how can it solve their challenges? What's in it for them? Dangle these beauties in their faces. But that's not enough, remember that nagging question you need to ask yourself? *So what?*
- **Desire** – Now you need to dig deeper and hook them with your *emotional benefits*. They now know that they need you, but it's time to make them *want* you, too. Paint a picture of how your product can help them reach their dreams and aspirations. Present further proof or a bigger reason to buy in. This is the point that makes them go *I need this in my life now, just shut up and take my money!!!*
- **Action** – And finally, simply tell them what to do so they can finally take home the product or service of their dreams.

PAS

PAS, on the other hand, is the more mischievous of the two ladies. While AIDA focuses on your customers' dreams and aspirations, PAS thrives on their fears and nightmares. She's highly effective in her craft as more than wanting some good every now and then, people definitely want to avoid something bad at all cost!

PAS stands for Problem, Agitate, Solution, and this is how she operates:
- **Problem** – Open your proposal with a problem. What's your persona's biggest pain point? That will

be your selling point. People will do anything to avoid any hassle, pain, or headache. So, remind them of their problem!

- **Agitate** – Next, amplify that problem. Add salt to the wound, and fuel to the fire. Use power words that trigger fear and anger. Make their frustrations larger than life and just before they lose it...
- **Solution** – Present yourself as the solution. Paint a picture of how much greener the grass is on your side, and how wonderful life can be if they only take that one last step to end their nightmare... Which is to finally close the deal with you.

Tricky, isn't she? But imagine how much more powerful your copy can be when these two ladies work together.

Drill #5

Here's an example of a landing page from Basecamp. Can you identify which formula they used?

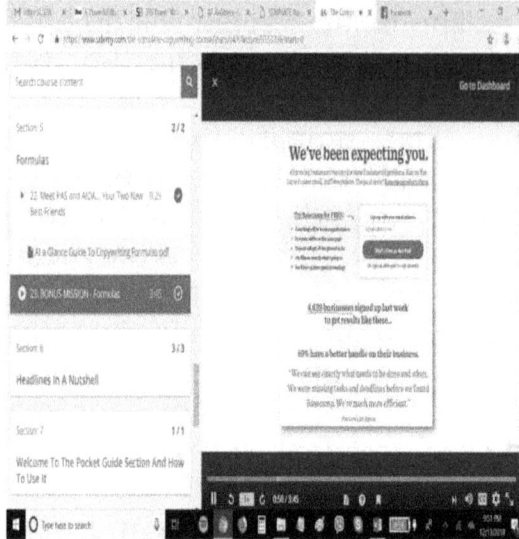

Yup, that was a trick question. This sample makes use of both formulas! So, as you can see, you can use them for anything from a headline, to an ad, an EDM, a splash page, and so on.

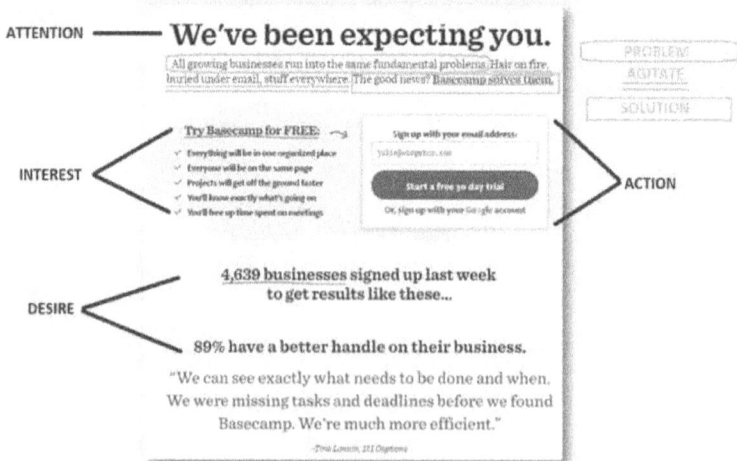

Who run the world? These girls certainly, do. And while there are many other formulas out there, they're mostly just variations of AIDA and PAS.

Try creating sample copies for the same mobile phone in the previous exercises. Write one sample using the AIDA formula, one sample using the PAS formula, and one sample combining both!

What's important for you to remember is that formulas are fluid and flexible. They're just basic principles of how you can shape or layout your copy – But what you say, is still more important than how you say it.

You can have the boldest headline, sell the most appealing benefits, or highlight the most frustrating problems. But if what you're saying doesn't resonate with who's reading it, your perfectly crafted copy won't give you the conversions you need. It all still boils down to how much you understand your persona, and how relevant your copy is to them.

The You Language

"People aren't interested in you, they're interested in themselves."

– Dale Carnegie

Whether you're writing copy for your own business or for a client, and whether you choose to follow the AIDA or the

PAS formula, don't forget exactly who your copy is intended for – your target audience.

What would they want to hear or read?
Why should they listen to you?
What's in it for them?

Reverse the roles and evaluate yourself as a consumer. How do you choose which ads, social media posts, or articles you pay attention to?

Let's say you're visiting New Jersey for the first time and stumble upon a list of the best restaurants in town. Which of these two are you most likely to check out first?

Restaurant 1:
We're one of New Jersey's finest restaurants, offering the best pizzas in town. Our award-winning dishes are from our own family recipes, passed down from generation to generation. Visit us for authentic Italian cuisine. We look forward to welcoming you into our home!

Restaurant 2:
Are you searching for the best pizza in town? You're welcome to visit our home for a taste of authentic Italian cuisine. Our award-winning dishes are from our own family recipes, passed down from generation to generation. One bite and you'll discover why we're one of Jersey's finest restaurants!

Based on the psychology of consumers and best marketing practices, Restaurant 2 should be more effective. Why? It's because of simply shifting the focus from the business, to the customer.

Let's go back to the quote shared earlier – people are interested in themselves. Put yourself in your target audience's shoes and focus on what they want. Both examples are technically saying the same thing, but the second restaurant utilizes the YOU language.

By simply using more YOUs, and less Is or WEs, you have more chances of building an instant connection with your reader. Filling your copy with Is and WEs is like that friend who keeps talking about themselves at the party, and won't even bother to ask how you're doing. It's one-way, distant, and can get really annoying, fast.

Drill #6

Here's an example of the copy written for the "About Us" section of website.com, a company offering web development services:

> We believe everyone deserves to have a website or online store. Innovation and simplicity make us happy: our goal is to remove any technical or financial barriers that can prevent business owners from making their own website. We're excited to help you on your journey!

Try adding more YOUs and tweaking the overall copy to make it more conversational. Even if it's "About Us," your job as a copywriter is to somehow still make it about your customers. Something like this would build a better connection:

You deserve to have a website or online store. If innovation and simplicity make you happy, then we're on the same page. Our goal is to remove any technical or financial barriers that can prevent you from making your own website. We're excited to help you on your journey!

Rather than putting the spotlight on the company, and talking about conceptual customers (they), why not speak directly to your market? Even if you're talking to the general public, readers would appreciate and respond more if they feel like your copy is intended specifically for them. Make your readers feel special.

Here's another example:

Our clients put thought into the products they make, the items they sell, the blog articles they write, or the software they build. We believe that makes us a good fit for each other. Our clients care deeply about the products and/or services they offer. It is safe to say that quality is their top priority. Doing what we love lies on finding the right client partners. We are dedicated to finding the ideal people to work with. People who put importance on their craft, design, value our input, and are authentic individuals. It is unfortunate that we have to turn down many potential work, as we have to decline the wrong fit, allowing us to work with the right fit. That's how we're able to come in each day with smiles on our faces.

Sounds like a great company that's very proud of their current customers – but as a prospective client, I'm not quite sure if I'm welcome to get in touch with them... Try rewriting this in the You Language and see what happens.

As our client, we value how much thought you put into the pizza you make, the tea you sell, the blog you write, or the software you build. That's what makes us a good fit together. You care deeply about the products you offer or the services you provide, and quality is your top priority. Doing what we love hinges on finding the right client partners, so we're dedicated to finding the ideal people to work with – clients like you who value your craft, value design, value our input, and also happen to be nice, genuine humans. This means we turn down a lot of potential work – we say no to the wrong fit, so we can say yes to the right fit – and we hope, that's you. So, we can both go to work each day with smiles on our faces.

See how much warmer, inviting, and more engaging it is now? I'd much rather talk to these guys than the ones earlier!

Who knew three letters could make such a drastic difference to your copy? Remember, copywriting isn't meant to be a monologue. Don't just talk. Talk to your customers, and give them a chance to respond with a conversion.

Coffee Talks

Here's another technique to keep your copy in check – talk to your customers as if you're chatting with a friend in a coffee shop.

Imagine this: You're at your neighborhood café, totally chill, enjoying your cup of joe, and settling in to start working on your copy. You suddenly see a familiar face walk by – It's a buddy you haven't seen in a while. You immediately invite them over and start catching up. *"What are you up to? What are you working on?"*, they ask. You tell them about the upcoming launch and they're interested to know more about this new phone. *"Oh cool, tell me more about it!"* How would you answer them? What would your conversation be like? Hold that thought – We'll get back to this later.

Write Like You Speak
Conversational writing is quickly becoming the language in business as well. With the power and prevalence of social media, the wall between brands and customers have been broken. The more accessible, sociable and personable your brand voice is, the better.

Write about your product or service as if you're explaining it to a friend. Remember how excited you were about something you've been dying to buy, and you told your friends all about how cool it was, and why you needed it in your life? Hold on to that thought and replicate it in your copy.

Keep it casual, even if you're trying to sell a serious product.

Here's how:
- Even if your copy is intended for thousands of people, only write for one person. This goes back to the *You Language* – make each reader feel like you're just talking to them, and they have your full attention.

40

- Keep it simple. Use short sentences and avoid complex words. This will make your copy easier to absorb. When you're done writing, review your work and try replacing bigger words with simpler ones. Copywriting isn't a vocabulary contest – It's not about using the best words you know, but the words your customer understands.
- Like in any good conversation, keep it two-way and ask questions. This also helps you avoid the *Me, Myself and I* type of writing, and makes your copy more engaging.
- Your English teacher might hate you for this, but go ahead and make use of contractions. This keeps your copy fluid and natural. Use *let's, you're, aren't...* Otherwise, you'll sound like a robot.

When you're done writing, here's the one thing you must do to truly nail a convincing, non-salesy copy: Read it out loud. This is the best way to check your overall tone and flow. If it sounds like something you'd naturally say – awesome!

Drill #7

Let's go back to the coffee shop scene. How would you tell your friend about this new phone that your client will launch next month? Start writing. Imagine what their follow-up questions might be, and continue writing. See where your conversation takes you, and read it out loud.

Conversations Lead to Conversions

Who are you most likely to listen to? Someone you met at a party telling you about a new phone they heard about, or the sales guy at the phone shop telling you about their new product launch next month?

Writing your copy should be as effortless as slipping it in a conversation at a party. It's not hard sell, not aggressive, no salesy at all. Consumers have evolved and appreciate being treated as a peer or a friend, as opposed to just being one of the many anonymous receivers of your message.

Conversational copy makes your writing more genuine, personal, and engaging, so it helps you build rapport with your target audience. It' a lot easier to understand, too, especially for long formats (like an e-book!).

So, when in doubt, go back to your imaginary coffee shop. Talk to your imaginary friend and see how your copy fits in your conversation.

CHAPTER 4: THE BATTLEFIELD

It's time to put your new-learned skill to the test.

You're now armed with the fundamentals and trade secrets of copywriting. While everything you've learned so far are basic principles for any type of copy, some guidelines may be more applicable than others for
specific copy requirements.

In this chapter, you'll try your hand at copy-specific drills. Consider this as a refresher course when you're about to take on a certain type of material. Some of the tips in the following pages may seem repetitive at times – Again, they're mere reminders of how you can best apply what you've learned in *The Boot Camp* and *The Big Guns*. Once you've nailed down those two chapters, it's much easier to see how you can apply certain strategies and tactics to different types of copy.

For each exercise, remember your training:
- Map out your plan of action first. Create a persona, identify your product benefits, translate these to emotional benefits with power words, and craft a compelling call to action.
- Choose a formula to follow and write in conversational style using the You Language.
- Read your copy out loud, and revise as needed.

You can now unload all the knowledge you've stashed in your armory.

Ready. Aim. Fire!

Ads and Headlines that Stick

First impressions last. And with any copy, your first sentence should stick – attract, entice, seduce your reader to click, read, open or share.

Headlines – well – head line your ads, social media posts, articles and just about everything else you write. Your opening statement has one goal: To get your first sentence read. Your body copy shall do the rest.

Here are the Four Effective U's to help you get started. Make sure your headline ticks one of these boxes:

- **Urgent** – A sense of urgency in your ad or article's headline helps make sure that they get noticed and acted on *now*, instead of having it saved for later. Coz let's face it – Even with Facebook's save feature, or your browser's bookmark function, you often forget to get back to them later. Use your explosive power words and pepper your headline with *today, right now, quick, asap* or *this summer* – and highlight what your readers might miss out on if they don't act *this instant*.

- **Unique** – Write in a fresh and surprising way. If it suits your product's brand voice, be as creative as you want to be. Take Buzzfeed's headlines for example. Instead of simply saying *The Top Ten Shows This Season* they might say something along the lines of *Binge-worthy Shows You Should Def Watch This Weekend Coz You Don't Have a Life* or *Top Ten*

Shows This Season for People Who Crave More Drama in their Life – That's You BTW.

- **Ultra-specific** – This one takes its cue from *How to Lose a Guy in 10 Days* and your usual *Lose 10 lbs in 14 Days.* People love being offered something quick and easy. Again, your role is to be the bearer of good news and the answer to their biggest problems. While *How to be a Successful Entrepreneur* presents a good solution, *How to be A Successful Entrepreneur, Be Your Own Boss and Quit Your Job in 30 Days* definitely sounds better!

- **Useful** – Sometimes, all you need to do is offer help. No tricks, no buzzwords, just an honest to goodness solution. It boils down, once again, to how much you know your persona, so your simple yet useful headline can resonate strongly with them. *5 Time Management Tools to Help you be More Productive at Work,* or *Simple Exercises You Can Do Even While Sitting Down* could be all they really need right now.

Once you've determined which of these U's would suit your copy requirements best, here are a few other tips to make sure you never write a boring headline again!
- Ask a question. It grabs attention and makes your reader want to read some more to find the answer.
- Include numbers. They're eye-catching and can break a monotonous headline.

- Make a bold claim. Again, your copy's all about being *the* solution your customers have been dying for. Own it!
- But, don't go for clickbait. Don't overpromise in your headline then underdeliver in the rest of your content. You need to build a genuine connection.
- Write at least 20 headlines. It's great exercise to get your creative juices flowing. See what you come up with, which one you like best, or perhaps, you can even mix and match some lines to zone in on your winning headline!

Drill #8

Rewrite the following headlines in four ways: Make each one an urgent, a unique, an ultra-specific, and a useful version, and try incorporating the other tips above!
- Parents Tweet the Darndest Things
- The Top Ten Must Try Restaurants in Town
- The App You've Been Waiting for Your Whole Life is Finally Here

Emails that Make You Click

Standing out in an over-crowded inbox is a challenge. Just imagine how many newsletters your target customers have signed up for – and how many offers, reminders, and notifications they receive each day. How can you make them notice you?

Here are some best practices on how you can get your recipients to open, read, and click on your email:

- **Make the most of your subject.**
  Similar to a headline, your email's subject should make a great first impression. Keep it simple, but descriptive and straight to the point. Avoid any sales jargon, buzz words, and spammy words such as *sale*, *help* and *percent*. Most of all, don't use a clickbait that has nothing to do with the content of your email. Spend time thinking, writing and revising your subject – Make it sound like an email from a friend.

- **Choose formulas over templates.**
  Email templates force you to adhere to their format, while formulas are much more fluid and can be tailored for your specific audience. Remember AIDA and PAS? Emails are one of the best channels to use them as you have more room to talk about benefits and solutions. See which one fits your product or email campaign better.

- **Be personal.**
  Simply addressing your recipient goes a long way. *Hi [name]* is most likely to get your

customer scrolling and reading more, as opposed to opening with *Hi everyone*. Remember – write as if you're just talking to one person, and make each customer feel special. If you write to everyone, you write to no one. Use the You Language and keep the rest of your email body casual, much like a natural conversation. All The Big Guns play a crucial role here! It also helps if the sender has a name, instead of just the company name.

- **Keep it concise.**
  You may feel tempted to keep rambling in an email, thinking you have more space and time, compared to an ad for example. Despite of its more flexible medium, however, it's still best to keep your email copy short and straight to the point. Any sales copy is meant to propose a solution, remember? So best to get to that part right away. If you have lots of copy points to cover, use bullet points – It will be much easier for your reader to absorb everything at a glance.

- **Repeat your call to action.**
  Don't be afraid to repeat your call to action. Many businesses make the mistake of only leaving a button at the bottom or end of an email. If you can integrate this at the start and main body of your email as well, all the better. It doesn't always have to be the same button, too – find other ways of phrasing the same CTA. You already had some practice earlier, you got this!

Write a sample EDM inviting your target customers to the launch of your client's new phone. Incorporate the tips shared above – Be sure to have a couple of subject options, and have a personal, concise, and conversational email body with an effective formula and compelling calls to action.

You may have heard or encountered other email marketing tips such as the character limit for your subject, or when the best time for an email blast is. But here's the most important thing to remember – Copywriting is a social science based on human behavior. There are no one-size-fits-all template to follow. The best thing you can do is try out different tactics, keep testing, and see which is most effective for your brand and target market.

When everything's said and done, copywriting really is about a lot of practice. Just keep writing, testing, and learning, and forming compelling sales copy will eventually come easily and intuitively to you.

Product Descriptions that Sell

Describing a product seems like a pretty simple task. All you have to do is see, touch, smell, hear or taste it. As a copywriter, you're also often provided with reference materials to help you flesh out your copy. Even a paperclip can be described in various ways – its size, color, flexibility, material used, and so on. The challenge, however, is in making your paperclip *the* paperclip that your customer should buy.

When it comes to product descriptions, it's often tempting to simply list down all the technical specs. How many e-commerce websites have you encountered that just show you all the product features? It's great to know that Blanket A has a higher thread count than Blanket B, or that Refrigerator A is an Inverter, and Refrigerator B isn't – but what does that mean exactly?

In Chapter 2, we discussed the difference between product features and benefits, and how the latter leads to a greater emotional hook. It's this hook that provides a better chance for conversion.

In this section, we'll revisit the Boot Camp once again and explore other effective methods for writing compelling product descriptions.

- **Focus on your buyer.**
  Always keep your persona in mind. Imagine selling your product to them face-to-face, or just having a conversation with them at a coffee shop. What's their language – their humor, expressions, tone and personality? What would their questions be? How would they react to your answer? Take that conversation to your website and apply it on your product descriptions.

- **Translate your product features to benefits.**

As a copywriter, it's important to fully immerse yourself in the brand or business you're writing for. Chances are you've written other types of copy for them, you know their products or services by heart, and their jargon and technical features have been your second language. Problem is, this may be totally alien to your customer. List down each feature of your product, and write a corresponding benefit that would resonate with your target buyer. How can each feature benefit them in their daily lives or current frustrations?

- **Don't just sell the product, sell the experience.**
  Avoid relying on salesy phrases such as *superior quality* or *the best in the market*. As soon as your market sees this, it's easy for them to dismiss your copy as just another pitch they've seen from other products before. It's a generic claim. Be specific. Paint a clear picture of the possibilities of how much easier, happier, or more successful their lives can be because of your product feature. Instead of simply mentioning that this shampoo has green tea extract, this facial wash has acne-combatting ingredients, or this toothpaste has intense peppermint flavor that lasts...Sell the promise of confidence.

- **Support your claims.**
  Highlighting the benefits doesn't mean disregarding the specs and features. It's best to have a combination of both, where the features support the benefits. If you claim to

be the fastest, the strongest, or the most advanced – Prove it. Write your benefits in the most enticing way, then back it up with your list of features. Having testimonials on your product page is also a great way to do this, especially if it includes an image of the reviewer, or a snippet from social media.

- **Tease your customer's imagination.**
It's a lot easier to sell a product your customers can see, touch, and test. Unfortunately, you don't have this privilege when writing product descriptions for the web. Great news is, you can always appeal to their imagination. Flex those copywriting muscles. Go back to your power words, and combine these with sensory words. Make your copy as descriptive, detailed and vivid as possible. Start with *imagine* and fill the rest of your copy with words like *crunchy*, *crisp, smooth, velvety, rich*. These will definitely help your readers have a taste of your product, or experience your service, even if it's just through their screens.

Different products may present different challenges, but the basic principles of an effective sales copy will always take you back to The Boot Camp. Simply understand your persona and sell them a powerful emotional benefit.

Website Copy that Converts

A website is now every brand's most important digital asset. It's a hub of all the information they need their target audience to know. For location-based businesses, it's an extension of their physical shop. Whether it's a simple portfolio website of specialized services or an e-commerce site of various products, the goal isn't to fill it with as much information as possible. It's to convert.

The key to writing persuasive web copy is clarity. From how you structure your content, to your choice of words, your visitors need to understand exactly what you're trying to say, where you want them to click, and what you want them to do. Here's how:

- **Write for your target audience.**
  Yes, as always, you need to start writing by going back to your persona. This is the only way you can craft your copy to give them exactly what they're looking for, in a way that's specifically easy for them to absorb. Different audiences have different needs, questions, priorities, tone of preference and trigger words – and your website copy should adjust accordingly.

- **Be a trust-worthy problem-solver.**
  The more you know about your customer, the more you can anticipate their problems and concerns. Welcome them to your site with your solution. Focus on your features and benefits, and address any bottlenecks they may have. You can do this by integrating elements that build trust such as testimonials, reviews, case studies, press coverage, and product ratings. You can also throw in risk-free offers in your call to action such as *cancel anytime*, *free trial*, and *money back guarantee.* All these features

will ease your web visitors and help them overcome any doubts or hesitations they may have.

- **Get to the point.**
  You only have three seconds to hook your web visitors when they land on your website. Instead of opening with a witty headline just for the sake of being witty, or some splashy animation, present your most important copy points right away. Help your visitors find what they need, as quickly as possible. An overly animated or cluttered website may chase away potential customers who simply need an immediate answer. Also stick with short and simple, yet clever and creative copy. No industry jargon and no complex words. When in doubt, it's always safe to imagine that you're reading your website copy to grade school kids.
- **Keep it conversational.**
  As discussed in Chapter 3, even if a website is technically about a business, you should shift the attention to your customers and find a way to still make it seem about them. Talk to them, always utilize the YOU Language and avoid Is, WEs and THEYs. Go back to the coffee shop scene, and imagine having a casual chat with them. Keep the conversation two-way – Ask questions, which immediately prompts an interaction.

- **Show personality.**
  Your website will serve as your best representation online. Even if your copy is

focused on your customers, you can still show your brand's personality in your writing style. Determine your overall tone and brand voice, and keep it consistent throughout your site. Aside from your products and services, it's your personality that will set you apart from your competition and allow you to make a good impression.

Web Content Formatting Guidelines

Aside from keeping your copy clear and customer-driven, here are a few other formatting guidelines to help shape your copy for higher conversions:

- Consider scanability and write for skimmers by breaking down your content into headings and sub headings.
- Try to keep your paragraphs to four sentences or less.
- Try to keep your sentences to twelve words or less.
- Include links to other pages of your website, especially your goal URLs or conversion pages.
- Always clearly tell your visitors what to do next – *click here, download now, sign-up today* – and apply tips on writing compelling calls to action.

Onsite SEO

It's no secret that writing for the web is ruled by keywords. It's definitely recommended that you integrate your target keywords in your copy – but do so in the most natural way. Only include them if they seamlessly fit in the conversation. Never insert keywords just for the sake of having them there.

Here's a rule of thumb when it comes to optimizing your copy – Write for your readers first, and Google second. Don't get hung up on SEO writing guidelines. Always focus on your reader. They're online searching for solutions. The more you appeal to your customers and give them the content they need, they more you'll appeal to Google's algorithm. Always ask yourself, *How else can I be more helpful to my reader?* If you address this correctly, your website's conversion and optimization will follow.

Landing Pages that Hit the Mark

In the previous section, we talked about general web copy guidelines to help convert your web visitors to customers. While any sales copy should focus on conversion, landing pages are specifically created just for this purpose.

By now, you've already mastered the basic principles of conversion-driven copy. So, in this section, we'll tackle specific copy points for you to focus on when A/B testing your landing pages.

- **Your headline** – Go back to the different headline styles you've learned. Try a different style, or try replacing your power words. Add some numbers, or more creative phrases. You could also try switching your bold statement with a question instead. Write 20 more options, assess, mix and match, and test. Remember, you need to start strong to allow the rest of your copy to do their job.

- **Your call to action** – Is your CTA clear, enticing enough, and evident? Similar to your headline, you may want to try different styles and power words as well. Perhaps you could make it sound more urgent, or throw in a risk-free offer? Or sometimes, this may not even be a copy issue. See if modifying your CTA button may do the trick. Perhaps its style, color, or position may need some adjustment? It could all boil down to the smallest detail, such as your choice of font!

- **The amount of information provided** – Compared to the rest of your website copy, your landing page should focus on content for a specific campaign. Perhaps it's too concise and you haven't provided enough information to convince them of your product's value? Or maybe there's too much information for them to process? Review the significance of every copy point you have, and assess if there's anything missing or irrelevant. Again, this could also boil down to design and layout. Is it too cluttered? Is there a better way to visually present all the information you have?

- **Possible objections** – Revisit your persona. Review the bottlenecks you identified or possible objections to using your product or service. Were you able to address them in your landing page? Are there other possible sources of hesitation that you can think of? Or perhaps you're not addressing their most pressing concern?

- **Trust elements** – Are there enough trust elements in your landing page? Should you make the testimonials or ratings more evident? Is there a new review from a credible source that you can feature? Are your trust elements believable and easy to verify? Or are there better testimonials that you can use? Perhaps the ones you have now aren't really addressing your persona's main challenges, or they just seem to be generic statements?

Landing pages can be tricky. The problem and solution may either lie in your copy, on the overall layout, design, or a combination of different elements. What's important to remember is to test, and test some more. You may think that your landing page is already performing well, but you wouldn't really know unless you try changing different variables, and see how that affects your conversion. There might not even be a problem, but just other ways to make it better!

Conclusion

Congratulations! You're now licensed to kill... in copywriting, of course.

In a nutshell, good copy puts the customer first, and presents an immediate solution as effortlessly as possible, to persuade them to take a specific action.

It starts with understanding your target audience – their needs, wants, and challenges – which often requires not just a practical, but an *emotional* answer.

Highlight a benefit instead of product specifications, focus on value instead of price, and trigger emotion instead of just reason. This is where the power of words comes into play.

Know the challenges you can solve, understand the bottlenecks you need to overcome, and revel in the dreams you can help fulfill – That's how you accomplish your mission.

Thanks for Reading!

What did you think of, **Killer Copywriting, How to Write Copy That Sells**

I know you could have picked any number of books to read, but you picked this book and for that I am extremely grateful.

I hope that it added at value and quality to your everyday life. If so, it would be really nice if you could share this book with your friends and family by posting to Facebook and Twitter.

If you enjoyed this book and found some benefit in reading this, I'd like to hear from you and hope that you could take some time to post a review. Your feedback and support will help this author to greatly improve his writing craft for future projects and make this book even better.

I want you, the reader, to know that your review is very important and so, if you'd like to leave a review, all you have to do is click here and away you go. I wish you all the best in your future success!

The Free Offer

Do you want to boost your sales, save time and grow your business at a lightning speed?

Start Now, and Take Your Copywriting to The Next Level

http://killercopy.ontrapages.com/

www.ingramcontent.com/pod-product-compliance
Lightning Source LLC
Chambersburg PA
CBHW031910200326
41597CB00012B/572